Padre Pio

*Encounters and Miraculous Healings - A
Journey Through the Life of a Modern Saint*

Written by Saul Cross

Padre Pio

Encounters and Miraculous Healings - A Journey Through the Life of a Modern Saint

Copyright 2023. Motmot.org

All rights reserved. No part of this book may be reproduced or used in any manner without the prior written permission of the copyright owner, except for the use of brief quotations.

To request permission, contact the publisher by visiting the website: motmot.org.

Included Bonuses

Your purchase includes two e-books that you can read from any device.

» The Prayers of the Saints

» The Spiritual Exercises by St. Ignatius of Loyola

Scan the following QR code to visit our website and obtain the included material:

———————— or ————————

Visit us at https://motmot.org/85

Contents

Preface 10

The Life of Padre Pio 14
    Early Life 15
    Education & Formation 17
    Adult Life & Ministry 19
    Death 21
    Canonization and Legacy 23
    The Path to Canonization 23
    Canonization Process 23
    The Canonization Ceremony 24

Miracles and Wonders 26
    Recoveries 29
    Bilocation 34
    Odor of Sanctity 36
    Levitation 38
    Apparitions 40
    Encounters with the Devil 42
    Clairvoyance 44
    Confession 46

Feast Day and Liturgical Celebrations of Padre Pio 48
    Significance of the Feast Day 49

    Holy Mass … 49
    Novenas and Prayers … 50
    Processions and Veneration of Relics … 50
    Acts of Charity and Service … 50
    Educational and Cultural Events … 51
    Pilgrimages … 52
    Sharing Stories of Padre Pio's Intercession … 52

Prayers and Devotions … 54
    Healing Prayers … 55
    Family & Relationship Prayers … 59
    Spiritual Growth Prayers … 63
    Financial Prayers … 67
    Protection and Safety Prayers … 71
    Novena … 75

Afterword … 82

Appendix … 84
    Places of Pilgrimage and Veneration … 85
    Important relics and their locations … 86
    Pilgrimage traditions … 87
    Lessons and Reflections … 89
    Popular Quotes … 91

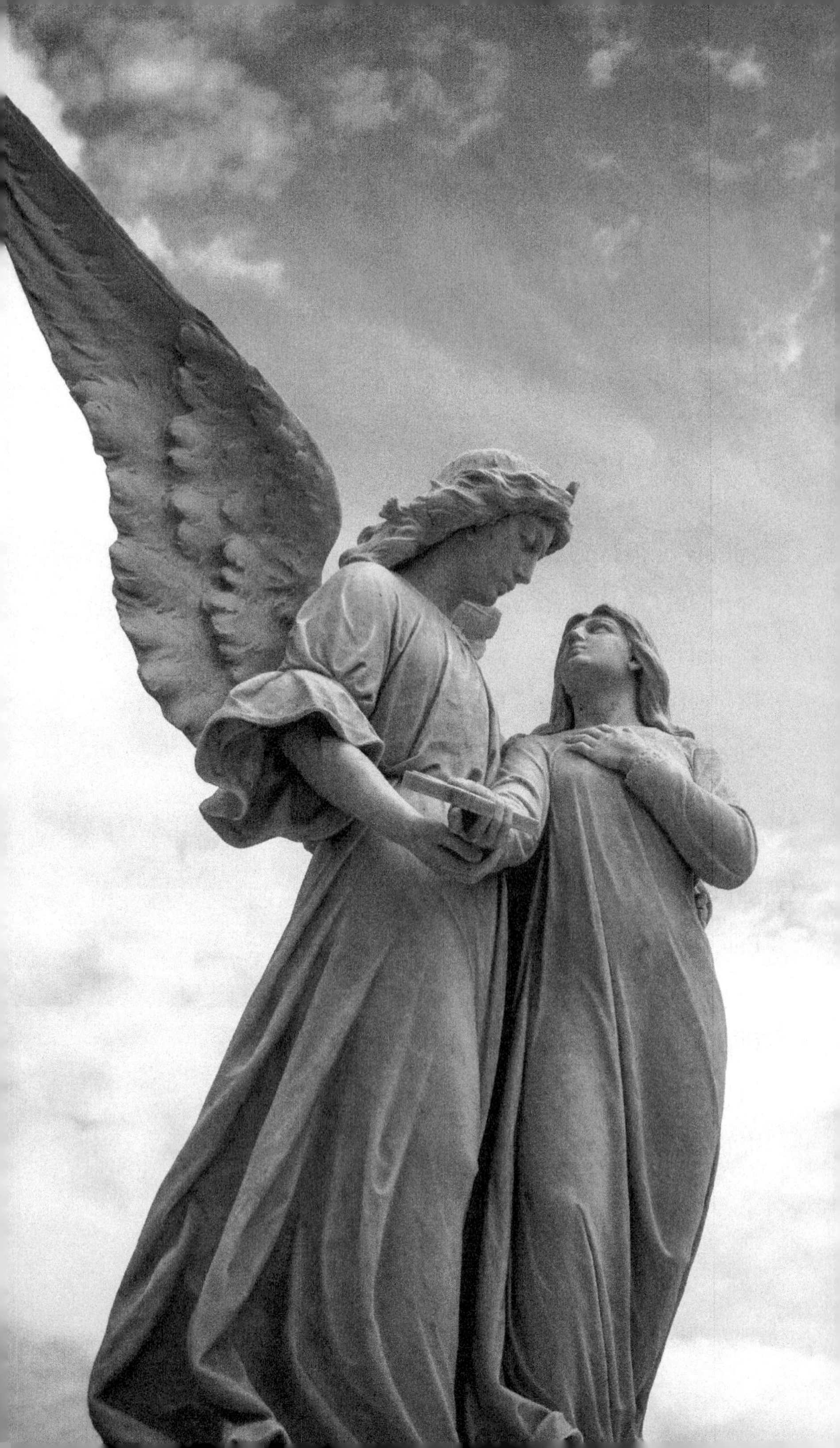

"Things that are seen are temporary, but things that are not seen are eternal."

2 Corinthians 4:18

Preface

In our fast-paced, ever-evolving world, stories of faith and unwavering devotion often seem like relics from a bygone era. But every so often, a figure emerges whose life and legacy provide a bridge between the divine and the human, challenging us to re-examine our understanding of spirituality and resilience. Padre Pio is one such figure. Through his humility, dedication, and miraculous healings, Padre Pio has left an indelible mark on the lives of countless individuals across the globe.

This book, "Padre Pio: Encounters and Miraculous Healings - A Journey Through the Life of a Modern Saint," invites you on a journey through the life and legacy of a modern saint who has touched the hearts and souls of many. We will delve into his early life, education, and formation, and explore his adult life and ministry, which were marked by astonishing miracles and profound spiritual insights.

As we recount the story of Padre Pio's death and subsequent canonization, we will also examine the impact his life has had on the Catholic Church and the world at large. We will explore the numerous miracles attributed to him, as well as the prayers and devotions that have sprung up in his name. We will visit the places of pilgrimage and veneration that have become sanctuaries for the faithful, and learn about the relics and pilgrimage traditions associated with this extraordinary saint.

In the chapters that follow, we will also offer lessons and reflections drawn from Padre Pio's life and teachings. These insights, alongside popular quotes from the saint himself, serve as a reminder of the power of faith and the beauty of a life dedicated to serving others.

Our hope is that this book will not only inform you about the remarkable life of Padre Pio, but also inspire you to contemplate your own spiritual journey. Through his example, we can glean valuable lessons about resilience, compassion, and the importance of living a life grounded in faith.

As you embark on this journey with us, may the story of Padre Pio's life serve as a beacon of hope, illuminating the path toward spiritual growth and a deeper understanding of the divine.

Welcome to the extraordinary world of Padre Pio.

The Life of Padre Pio

Early Life

Born on May 25, 1887, in the small Italian town of Pietrelcina, Francesco Forgione was the fourth of eight children. His parents, Grazio Orazio Mario Forgione and Maria Giuseppa di Nunzio, were simple, hardworking, and deeply devout people. Their unwavering faith would leave a lasting impression on young Francesco, shaping his spiritual journey from an early age.

Francesco's childhood home was modest, reflecting the family's humble socio-economic background. As an agriculturally-oriented household, his parents, alongside his siblings, worked tirelessly to make ends meet. Despite their meager resources, the Forgione family was rich in their love for God, with faith serving as the cornerstone of their daily lives.

From a young age, Francesco displayed a profound piety and deep connection to the divine. He often engaged in acts of penance, such as sleeping on a stone floor or fasting for extended periods. His childhood was marked by fragile health, suffering from various illnesses that would cause his body to weaken. Nevertheless, his spiritual strength remained unshaken, reflecting his unwavering devotion to God.

Francesco's desire to pursue the priesthood was sparked by an encounter with a Capuchin friar from the convent of Morcone, located 30 kilometers from Pietrelcina. The friar, named Brother Camillo, frequently visited the Forgione household to ask for alms. Witnessing the friar's humility and devotion profoundly impacted Francesco, inspiring him to follow in the footsteps of the Capuchin order.

To support his son's aspirations, Grazio Orazio Mario Forgione made the difficult decision to emigrate to the United States in 1898 and later to Argentina in 1910. His sacrifices allowed him to send financial assistance back home, enabling Francesco to pursue his religious education. The family's faith and determination ensured that Francesco's dream would become a reality.

Throughout his youth, Francesco experienced what he referred to as "demonic encounters." These episodes saw him grappling with seemingly supernatural forces, often appearing to fight his own shadow. Friends and neighbors testified to witnessing these unusual occurrences, which would accompany Padre Pio throughout his life.

One story that illustrates Francesco's early spiritual development involves an incident when he was just five years old. While tending to the family's sheep, he encountered a mysterious figure who identified himself as Jesus. The figure instructed Francesco to follow a life of devotion, obedience, and humility. This experience strengthened his desire to serve God and foreshadowed his future as a renowned spiritual leader.

Another formative event in young Francesco's life was when he received his first Holy Communion at the age of nine. Upon receiving the sacrament, he was overcome with emotion, feeling an intense connection to the divine. This moment confirmed his commitment to a life of religious devotion.

Education & Formation

The beginning of the year 1903 marked a significant milestone in the life of young Padre Pio. On January 6th, at the age of 15, he entered the convent of Morcone as a novice. Under the guidance of Father Tommaso da Monte Sant'Angelo, the novice master, Padre Pio embarked on his journey of spiritual growth and formation. Father Tommaso, described as a stern but compassionate teacher, played a crucial role in shaping the character and spirit of the young novices.

The novitiate period was a challenging time, filled with fasts and mortifications. These experiences helped the novices discern their true vocations and prepared them for a life of devotion. Despite his health struggles, which had plagued him since childhood, Padre Pio remained an exemplary novice throughout his time in the convent. The novice master attested to his unwavering commitment to the observance of the monastic rule.

Upon completing his novitiate on January 22, 1904, Padre Pio pronounced his temporary vows. Shortly thereafter, he moved to the convent of Sant'Elia to continue his studies. It was here that he experienced his first bilocation, attending the birth of Giovanna Rizzani in Venice despite being physically present in the convent.

Padre Pio professed his solemn vows on January 27, 1907, and was subsequently transferred to the convent of Serracapriola. Unfortunately, his health declined due to the coastal climate, prompting his superiors to send him back to his hometown of Pietrelcina for recovery. During this time, the townspeople sought his counsel, and he began guiding souls on their spiritual journeys.

In 1908, Padre Pio returned to monastic life, this time in Montefusco. Throughout that year, he received minor orders and the subdiaconate, immersing himself in prayer and study. His dedication to his faith culminated in his consecration as a priest on August 10, 1910, at the cathedral of Benevento.

Health challenges persisted, and Padre Pio remained with his family until 1916. During this period, he claimed to have received the stigmata. In September 1916, he was sent to the convent of San Giovanni Rotondo, where he would reside until his death. His service extended beyond the walls of the convent during World War I, as he served in the Italian Medical Corps from 1917 to 1918.

Padre Pio's journey of education and formation not only shaped his character but also laid the foundation for his spiritual leadership. Through the unwavering support of his mentors, the trials of the novitiate, and his own experiences with hardship, Padre Pio emerged as a devoted and compassionate servant of the Catholic faith.

Adult Life & Ministry

Padre Pio's adult life and ministry began in earnest when he returned to his monastic community in 1916. Despite ongoing health challenges, he proved to be a compassionate and dedicated servant of the Catholic faith.

In September 1916, Padre Pio was assigned to the Our Lady of Grace Capuchin Friary in San Giovanni Rotondo. He would remain in this community until his death in 1968, save for a brief period of military service during World War I. Padre Pio's deep commitment to his faith was evident in his spiritual practices and the guidance he provided to others. He was known to spend hours each day in prayer and contemplation, often meditating on the rosary. Padre Pio also emphasized the importance of regular confession, self-examination, and meditation in fostering spiritual growth.

As Padre Pio's reputation as a holy man grew, so too did the number of people who traveled to San Giovanni Rotondo to seek his guidance and intercession. He was widely regarded as a gifted spiritual director and confessor, and many who encountered him reported experiencing profound conversions and personal transformations. Padre Pio's ministry was marked by his dedication to the sacraments, his devotion to the rosary, and his encouragement of daily spiritual practices.

During World War I, Padre Pio served as a chaplain in the Italian army. He returned to San Giovanni Rotondo after being declared unfit for service due to his health. In September 1918, Padre Pio reportedly received the stigmata, which attracted even more attention to his ministry. Many people saw him as a symbol of hope and healing in the aftermath of the war, and they flocked to San Giovanni Rotondo to witness the extraordinary spiritual gifts that he was said to possess, such as healing, levitation, and prophecy.

Padre Pio's ministry was not without controversy, however. For a time, he was banned from celebrating Mass publicly and hearing confessions, but these restrictions were later lifted by Pope Pius XI and Pope Pius XII. By the mid-1960s, Pope Paul VI dismissed all accusations against Padre Pio, allowing his ministry to continue unimpeded.

One of Padre Pio's most enduring legacies is the establishment of the Casa Sollievo della Sofferenza (Home for the Relief of Suffering) hospital in San Giovanni Rotondo. Beginning as a small clinic in 1925, the hospital expanded significantly with the help of donations and contributions from various sources. Padre Pio's vision for the hospital was realized when it opened in 1956, providing much-needed medical care and relief to the suffering. Today, the Casa Sollievo della Sofferenza stands as a testament to Padre Pio's commitment to serving the needs of the sick and the poor.

Throughout his adult life and ministry, Padre Pio remained a steadfast servant of the Catholic faith, guiding countless souls along the path to spiritual growth and holiness. His profound devotion to prayer, the sacraments, and the care of the sick and suffering continues to inspire countless individuals, even many years after his death.

Death

As the sun set on the 22nd of September, 1968, the vibrant life of Padre Pio, a humble servant of God, was nearing its end. His final days were marked by physical weakness, but his unyielding spirit persevered in the face of adversity, much like it had throughout his extraordinary life. The dawn of the following day would witness the earthly departure of this beloved saint, who would soon be welcomed into the heavenly kingdom.

Padre Pio's final Mass was a testament to his enduring devotion to his divine calling. Despite his frailty, he mustered the strength to celebrate the sacred liturgy, commemorating the fiftieth anniversary of the miraculous stigmata that had marked his body for half a century. The gathered congregation, numbering in the thousands, bore witness to his unwavering faith and the tender love he held for both God and his fellow man.

Assisted by his fellow friars, Padre Pio completed his duties, his voice barely audible, his body trembling with exhaustion. Even in these final moments, he remained a beacon of hope and inspiration to those who had come to celebrate his life and ministry. As he descended the altar steps, his brothers in Christ gently supported him, a moving scene that would remain etched in the memories of all present.

On the morning of September 23, the sun rose to find Padre Pio in his cell, preparing for his final journey. With profound humility, he made his last confession and renewed his Franciscan vows, a testament to the unwavering devotion that had characterized his life. Clutching his rosary, he silently prayed, unable to voice the familiar Hail Marys. Instead, he whispered the names of Jesus and Mary, invoking their presence in his final moments.

As the clock struck 2:30 a.m., Padre Pio breathed his last, surrounded by the tranquility of his cell in San Giovanni Rotondo. The doctor who examined his lifeless body marveled at the sight before him; the wounds of the stigmata, which had accompanied Padre Pio for decades, were now completely healed, leaving no trace of their existence. It was a final, miraculous testament to the divine grace that had enveloped him throughout his life.

His earthly journey complete, Padre Pio's body was laid to rest in a simple coffin within the church of the monastery, providing an opportunity for the countless pilgrims who loved and admired him to pay their respects. On September 26, a solemn funeral ceremony was held, with an estimated 100,000 mourners in attendance. The streets of San Giovanni Rotondo were filled with the faithful, who came to bid farewell to their beloved Padre Pio.

Following the funeral procession and Mass, Padre Pio's body was interred in the crypt of the Church of Our Lady of Grace, a fitting resting place for one who had dedicated his life to the service of God and the spiritual well-being of his fellow man. Though Padre Pio had left this world, his legacy would continue to inspire and guide those who sought solace and guidance in the teachings of Christ. His heavenly homecoming marked not an end, but a new beginning for the countless lives he had touched.

Canonization and Legacy

Padre Pio's extraordinary life was marked by a deep spirituality, unwavering devotion to God, and a genuine compassion for the suffering of others. This chapter explores the process of Padre Pio's canonization, culminating in his elevation to sainthood within the Roman Catholic Church.

The Path to Canonization

The canonization process is a meticulous and lengthy procedure that the Catholic Church follows to recognize a person's sanctity and officially declare them a saint. Padre Pio's path to sainthood began with his death on September 23, 1968. After a waiting period of five years, as required by the Church, the cause for his beatification was introduced on March 20, 1983.

The diocesan phase of the investigation began in the Diocese of Rome, and over the years, testimonies from witnesses and a thorough examination of Padre Pio's life and writings were collected. The Congregation for the Causes of Saints reviewed the documentation, ensuring that Padre Pio's life exemplified the virtues of faith, hope, and charity, as well as the cardinal virtues of prudence, justice, fortitude, and temperance.

Canonization Process

One of the essential steps in the canonization process is the verification of miracles attributed to the intercession of the candidate for sainthood. Padre Pio was known for his supernatural gifts and his ability to heal, even during his lifetime. However, for his beatification and canonization, two posthumous miracles were required.

The first miracle, which paved the way for Padre Pio's beatification, was the healing of Consiglia De Martino, an Italian woman who suffered from a severe lung abscess. After praying for Padre Pio's intercession and keeping a relic of his glove near her chest, she experienced a sudden and inexplicable recovery. The medical board and theological commission of the Congregation for the Causes of Saints unanimously approved this miracle.

The second miracle, which led to Padre Pio's canonization, involved Matteo Pio Colella, a seven-year-old boy who was suffering from acute meningitis. His parents, both physicians, prayed fervently for Padre Pio's intercession. Miraculously, Matteo experienced a full recovery, astounding the medical community. Once again, the Congregation for the Causes of Saints confirmed the miraculous nature of the healing.

The Canonization Ceremony

On June 16, 2002, Pope John Paul II officially canonized Padre Pio, declaring him a saint of the Catholic Church. The canonization ceremony was attended by tens of thousands of devotees, many of whom had experienced Padre Pio's healing touch or spiritual guidance during their lives.

During the ceremony, Pope John Paul II praised Padre Pio's unwavering devotion to God and his extraordinary capacity to alleviate the suffering of others. The Pope stated, "The life and mission of Padre Pio testify that difficulties and sorrows, if accepted with love, transform themselves into a privileged journey of holiness, which opens the person toward a greater good, known only to the Lord."

The canonization of Padre Pio highlights the enduring impact of his life and his ability to inspire countless individuals in their quest for spiritual growth. Today, St. Pio of Pietrelcina continues to serve as a beacon of hope, faith, and compassion for millions of people worldwide.

Miracles and Wonders

Padre Pío's life was full of miracles, but it's essential to remember that the nature of a miracle is always divine. Padre Pío always encouraged people to give thanks to God, the true author of every miracle.

One of the first miracles attributed to Padre Pío occurred in 1908 when he lived in the Montefusco convent. He collected horse chestnuts in a bag to send to his loving aunt Daría. After eating the horse chestnuts and saving the bag as a keepsake, aunt Daría accidentally set her drawer on fire. She grabbed the bag containing Padre Pío's horse chestnuts and held it to her face. Instantly, her pain vanished, and no burn marks or wounds remained.

During World War II, bread was rationed in Italy. The convent where Padre Pío lived was always full of guests and poor people seeking food. One day, the friars found themselves with very little bread. After praying together, Padre Pío entered the church and returned with an abundance of bread, saying a pilgrim at the door had given it to him.

On one occasion at the convent, a friar forgot to organize enough people for Holy Communion. However, after hearing confessions, Padre Pío arranged for more people to participate, and the number of people exceeded the initial count.

A spiritual daughter of Padre Pío was reading a letter from him when the wind swept it away. The letter stopped beneath a rock, allowing the woman to retrieve it. When she met Padre Pío later, he told her to be more mindful of the wind and that he had placed his foot on the letter to prevent it from being lost.

During the Second World War, Cleonice, a spiritual daughter of Padre Pío, had a nephew who was a prisoner. His family hadn't heard from him in a year and believed he was dead. Cleonice wrote a letter to her nephew, addressing it only with his name, and asked Padre Pío to deliver it with the help of his guardian angel. The letter disappeared from her nightstand, and fifteen days later, her nephew replied.

Another miracle occurred during the Second World War when the son of a woman named Luisa, an officer in the British Royal Navy, was reported missing after his ship sank. Padre Pío consoled her, providing the exact name and address of the hotel where her son was staying after escaping the sinking ship. Luisa sent a letter, and her son replied fifteen days later.

Towards the end of Lent, a woman named Paolina was gravely ill. Her husband and five children prayed to Padre Pío for help. He promised to pray for them, but Paolina eventually died. However, as Padre Pío began to sing the Gloria during a mass, Paolina came back to life, saying she had ascended towards a great light before returning.

A mother testified that Padre Pío saved her daughter's life in 1955 when the child suffered severe burns. As the mother prayed to Padre Pío, her daughter called out, saying her wounds had vanished. The girl claimed that Padre Pío had healed her by placing his wounded hands on her burns.

During spring in San Giovanni Rotondo, almond trees promised a good harvest, but caterpillars devoured the leaves and flowers. The farmers turned to Padre Pío, who prayed and blessed the trees. The caterpillars disappeared, and the trees produced an abundant harvest, beyond any previous years.

Recoveries

Healings Attributed to Padre Pio

One of the most revered and beloved Catholic saints, Padre Pio, was known for his miraculous healings and intercessions. Many people who sought his help were granted astonishing recoveries, often defying the odds and baffling medical professionals. In this section, we will explore some of the most remarkable healing stories attributed to Padre Pio.

The Swollen Knee

A man experienced severe pain and swelling in his left knee, and his doctor recommended a series of injections. However, before starting the treatment, the man decided to visit Padre Pio. After confessing his sins and asking for prayers, the man noticed that his knee was no longer swollen or painful. He returned to Padre Pio to express his gratitude, but the saint simply replied, "You do not have to thank me, but you have to thank God!" and jokingly added, "Tell your doctor he can get the injections himself."

The Miraculous Recovery

In 1952, a woman experienced a complicated childbirth and required a blood transfusion. Unfortunately, she was given the wrong blood type, leading to severe health complications. As she lay on the brink of death, Padre Pio appeared to her in a vision, showing her his stigmatized hands and encouraging her to pray with him. The woman miraculously recovered, and the doctors acknowledged that a miracle had occurred. Padre Pio later told her, "You received a miracle, but you do not have to thank me. The Sacred Heart of Jesus sent me to rescue you because you are devoted to His Heart and you practiced the Nine First Fridays of the month."

The Vanished Illness

In 1953, a woman was diagnosed with a serious illness and required surgery. A friend suggested that she write a letter to Padre Pio, asking for his prayers and help. After receiving a response, the woman went to the hospital, where doctors discovered that her condition had inexplicably vanished. Forty years later, she was still grateful for Padre Pio's intervention.

The Crippled Railway-Man

A man suffered from a debilitating disease that left his legs immobilized. After years of unsuccessful treatments, his uncle suggested visiting Padre Pio. Upon meeting the saint, the man's legs were suddenly healed, and he was able to walk again. Astounded, his family attributed the miracle to Padre Pio.

The Cancer Miracle

In 1950, a woman was diagnosed with cancer and given only four months to live. After hearing about Padre Pio's miraculous powers, her son-in-law went to San Giovanni Rotondo and asked for the saint's help. Padre Pio assured him that the woman would recover, and she did – living for another nineteen years.

The Permanent Miracle

A railway-man suffered from a severely injured leg that doctors deemed incurable. Desperate, he and his wife traveled to see Padre Pio. After confessing to the saint and receiving his blessing, the man's leg was instantly healed, allowing him to walk again. This remarkable recovery astonished doctors, as his leg showed no signs of improvement on X-rays.

The Priest's Recovery

Sister Pagani visited Padre Pio to ask for his intercession for a priest suffering from lung cancer. Padre Pio initially hesitated, saying, "If God wants him to die, what can we do?" However, after some contemplation, he agreed to help. The priest recovered and was discharged from the hospital.

Pope Pio XII's Recovery

Between the end of 1953 and the beginning of 1954, Pope Pio XII experienced a physical breakdown due from these ailments came when he slept. His doctors were alarmed and tried to cure him, but their efforts were in vain." On February 6, 1954, the Pope's private secretary, Monsignor Domenico Tardini, informed Padre Pio of the Holy Father's poor health and requested prayers on his behalf. Padre Pio immediately sent a reply assuring him that he and his fellow friars would pray for Pope Pius XII's recovery. In a few days, the Pope's health had made a remarkable turnaround, and he was able to resume his duties. Monsignor Tardini wrote to Padre Pio, thanking him and his fellow friars for their prayers and expressing his deep gratitude.

Serious Illness

A gentleman recounted an incident that occurred in 1957: "My wife suffered from a serious illness for a long time. We visited many doctors, but none were able to diagnose her condition. We were desperate and lost hope. One day, a friend suggested we turn to Padre Pio for help. My wife wrote a letter to Padre Pio, explaining her situation and asking for his prayers. A few days later, my wife received a reply from Padre Pio, instructing her to go to a particular doctor in a nearby city. We went to the doctor, who was finally able to diagnose my wife's condition correctly. He prescribed a treatment plan, and within a short time, my wife was completely healed. We couldn't believe it! We returned to San Giovanni Rotondo to thank Padre Pio personally. He told us, 'It was God who healed her, not me. Always give thanks to Him.'"

Tumor During Pregnancy

In another instance, a woman from Naples shared her story: "In 1959, I was pregnant with my third child. Unfortunately, during the pregnancy, I developed a tumor in my uterus. The doctors told me that I needed an immediate operation, but there was a high risk of losing the baby. Devastated, I turned to Padre Pio for help. One night, as I lay in bed, I suddenly saw Padre Pio standing by my side. He said, 'Do not be afraid; everything will be fine. Trust in God and pray.' From that day on, I felt a renewed sense of hope and prayed fervently. When the time came for the operation, the doctors were amazed to find that the tumor had disappeared completely. My baby was born healthy, and I have never had any health issues since. I owe my life and my child's life to Padre Pio's intervention."

Tuberculosis

A man from Turin shared his experience: "In 1962, I was diagnosed with a severe form of tuberculosis. The doctors informed me that there was no cure and that I had only a few months to live. I was devastated, but my family urged me to seek Padre Pio's help. I wrote to him, asking for his prayers and intercession. Soon after, I experienced a powerful dream in which Padre Pio appeared to me. He placed his hands on my chest and said, 'You are healed.' When I awoke, I felt a great sense of peace and serenity. Miraculously, within a few days, my health began to improve. I returned to the hospital, and the doctors confirmed that I no longer had tuberculosis. To this day, I remain in good health and am forever grateful to Padre Pio."

These stories of miraculous healings attributed to Padre Pio's intercession are just a few among countless others. They demonstrate the incredible power of faith and prayer and the deep love that Padre Pio had for those who sought his help. Even though he always insisted that it was God who performed the miracles and healings, his role as an intercessor and the embodiment of God's love and mercy has left a lasting impact on the lives of many.

Bilocation

Bilocation, the astounding phenomenon of a person's simultaneous presence in two different places, has been a recurring theme in the lives of many saints throughout Christian history. Among these extraordinary individuals, Padre Pio is renowned for his unique gift of bilocation, with numerous eyewitness accounts testifying to his miraculous presence in different locations at the same time. In this chapter, we explore several testimonials that shed light on the remarkable instances of Padre Pio's bilocations.

Mrs. Maria, a spiritual daughter of Padre Pio, recounts an evening when her brother dozed off while praying. He was abruptly awakened by a slap on his cheek, delivered by a hand donning a half glove. Connecting the slap with Padre Pio, her brother inquired the next day, only to receive a light-hearted response from the saint, confirming his suspicions.

Another striking story comes from a former Italian Army Officer who recognized Padre Pio in the sacristy and tearfully thanked him for saving his life during a battlefield explosion. He had seen the friar urging him to move away from danger, moments before a grenade detonated in the very spot he had just vacated. Padre Pio's bilocation had saved the officer's life.

Father Alberto, who met Padre Pio in 1917, witnessed the saint's bilocation as he stood by a window, seemingly absorbed in a trance. Father Alberto later discovered that Padre Pio had blessed a dying man in Turin at that exact moment.

In 1946, an American bombardier plane pilot visited Padre Pio to thank him for saving his life during World War II. The pilot described how the saint had miraculously appeared midair, caught him in his arms, and gently set him down at the entrance of the base when his parachute had failed to open.

Other instances of bilocation include Padre Pio's visit to a woman suffering from a tumor in Bologna, his spiritual support to the Bishop who had ordained him, his appearance at the beatification of Saint Teresa in Rome, celebrating Holy Mass in Czechoslovakia and Budapest, and spending a year with Mother Speranza in Rome.

An Italian General, contemplating suicide after the defeat of Caporetto, was saved when Padre Pio appeared in his room, dissuading him from taking his own life. The saint's bilocation was also experienced by Father Agostino, who learned of Padre Pio's visit to a nun in Florence.

The final bilocation of Padre Pio occurred on September 22, 1968, when he visited Brother Umile in Genoa to bid him farewell. The following day, Padre Pio passed away, leaving a lasting impression on those who had been touched by his miraculous presence.

These compelling stories of Padre Pio's bilocations continue to inspire faith and awe in the hearts of believers. His remarkable gift, transcending the limitations of time and space, serves as a testament to the power of divine intervention and the enduring legacy of a truly extraordinary saint.

Odor of Sanctity

The gift of "odor of sanctity," or osmogenesia, has been attributed to various saints throughout history, with St. Padre Pio being one of the most prominent. This phenomenon is characterized by the presence of a unique, personal perfume that surrounds the saint, allowing others to perceive their presence through the powerful scent. St. Padre Pio was known for his own odors of holiness, which emanated not only from his body but also from the objects he touched or the places he passed through.

On one occasion, a doctor removed a blood-soaked bandage from Padre Pio's chest, placed it in a container, and brought it to his laboratory in Rome for analysis. During the journey, the other travelers accompanying the doctor reported smelling the distinct perfume that usually emanated from Padre Pio, although none of them knew about the gauze in the container. This perfume lingered in the doctor's laboratory, leaving patients questioning the source of the unusual aroma.

Friar Modestino recounted a similar experience. While serving at Padre Pio's Holy Mass, Modestino found himself overcome with the perfume of St. Pio. The scent grew so intense that it caused him to struggle with his breathing and almost faint. When asked about the phenomenon, Padre Pio admitted that he could not explain it, suggesting that God allowed the perfume to be smelled whenever He desired.

The power of Padre Pio's perfume reached far beyond the confines of his immediate presence. Many people reported encounters with the saint's distinct aroma during times of personal struggle, healing, or spiritual transformation. These experiences often served as signs of hope and reassurance, leading to miraculous changes in their lives.

One woman experienced the perfume after her husband's critical car accident. As she prayed to Padre Pio for his recovery, she was engulfed in the marvelous perfume of lilies. Her husband's condition soon improved, and he healed from his injuries. Another man, who had long avoided church, decided to visit Padre Pio for confession. After being initially rebuffed, he was suddenly overcome by the perfume, which led him to return to Padre Pio and receive the absolution he sought.

In another instance, a couple from England experiencing marital problems decided to travel to St. Giovanni Rotondo to seek Padre Pio's guidance. During their journey, they were overcome by the saint's perfume in a small hotel room, which they took as a sign to continue on their journey. Upon meeting Padre Pio, he confirmed that the perfume had indeed been a message from him, and he helped the couple resolve their issues.

These are but a few of the countless stories of people whose lives were touched by Padre Pio's odors of holiness. The powerful, mysterious perfume served as a testament to the saint's divine presence and his ability to reach out to those in need, providing comfort and guidance when it was most needed. In this way, the odor of sanctity became a profound symbol of the divine intervention that characterized Padre Pio's life and work, leaving a lasting impact on all who experienced it.

Levitation

Levitation, a phenomenon where a person lifts from the ground and remains suspended in mid-air, is a divine gift bestowed upon a select few mystics of the Catholic Church. St. Joseph of Copertino was well-known for his levitations, and Padre Pio of Pietrelcina was also blessed with this extraordinary gift. Witnesses reported numerous instances where Padre Pio was seen levitating above the earth.

During the Second World War, the American Air Forces General Command was stationed in Bari, Italy. Many officers credited Padre Pio with saving their lives during the war, including the General Commander who witnessed an incredible episode involving the mystic. The American Commanding Officer had planned to lead a squadron of bombers to destroy a German war material depot located in San Giovanni Rotondo. However, the General recounted that as the airplanes approached their target, he and his men saw a monk with uplifted hands in the sky. The bombs released on their own and fell into the woods, and the planes turned back without being maneuvered by the pilots or officers. Everyone wondered about the identity of the monk whom the aircraft had obeyed.

Upon learning about a miraculous monk residing in San Giovanni Rotondo, the General vowed to visit the Capuchin monastery after the war to see if this was the same monk they had encountered in the sky. Accompanied by some pilots, the General entered the sacristy and immediately recognized Padre Pio among the gathered monks. Padre Pio approached the General and asked, "Are you the one who wanted to kill all of us?" The General, moved by

Padre Pio's words and gaze, knelt before him. Although Padre Pio spoke in dialect, the General was convinced he had been addressed in English—a testament to another of Padre Pio's gifts. The two became friends, and the Protestant General eventually converted to Catholicism.

Another remarkable account of Padre Pio's levitation comes from Padre Ascanio. He recalled waiting for Padre Pio to hear confessions in a crowded church. Everyone's eyes were fixed on the door through which Padre Pio would enter, but instead, Padre Ascanio witnessed the saint walking above the heads of the congregation. He reached the confessional and vanished, only to reappear minutes later to receive penitents. Initially, Padre Ascanio kept this experience to himself, but later, he asked Padre Pio how he had managed to walk above the people. In a lighthearted tone, Padre Pio replied, "I can assure you, my child, it's just like walking on the floor..."

These miraculous levitations are just a few of the many instances that showcase Padre Pio's divine gifts. They serve as a testament to the extraordinary life of a saint who continues to inspire believers with his faith and devotion.

Apparitions

From a tender age, Padre Pio experienced apparitions of celestial beings, visions that he initially believed were normal occurrences for everyone. These apparitions included angels, saints, Jesus, and Our Lady, but also devils, who would challenge him in spiritual battles. These encounters shaped Padre Pio's life and prepared him for the trials he would face in his ministry.

In December 1902, young Francesco had a significant vision, which he later recounted to his confessor. In the vision, he was led by a bright, shining figure who encouraged him to fight against a monstrous, dark character. The shining figure assured him of divine assistance, promising that he would never be defeated. Francesco agreed, and with the help of the bright figure, he overcame the darkness. This vision foreshadowed the many struggles Padre Pio would face against the Devil throughout his life. His primary mission was to save souls from the clutches of evil.

Padre Pio had several encounters with souls from Purgatory, who sought his help to attain eternal rest. One such experience involved Pietro Di Mauro, a man who had died in a fire in 1908. Pietro appeared to Padre Pio, asking for a Mass to be said in his honor so he could enter Paradise. Padre Pio agreed, and the next day, the soul was released from Purgatory.

Another spiritual daughter of Padre Pio, Mrs. Cleonice Morcaldi, lost her mother. One month after her mother's passing, Padre Pio informed her that her mother had ascended to Heaven. Padre Pio's spiritual gifts allowed him to comfort the grieving and assure them of their loved ones' fates.

In another encounter, a young monk from Purgatory appeared to Padre Pio, seeking his help in expediting his entrance to Paradise. Padre Pio promised to say a Mass for him the following day, but the soul was disappointed, calling him cruel. Padre Pio realized that he had the power to release the soul immediately but had inadvertently sentenced him to another night of suffering.

Throughout his life, Padre Pio wrote letters to his spiritual father, detailing his experiences and visions. In one letter, he described Jesus' anguish over the ingratitude and indifference of humanity. In another, he shared Jesus' promise to strengthen and support him in times of temptation and trial.

As an older monk, Padre Pio continued to experience apparitions, including nightly visits from Our Lady. These divine encounters were a source of strength and guidance for him, as he continued to fight against the darkness and save souls from the grip of evil.

In this chapter, we explored the apparitions and spiritual battles that characterized Padre Pio's life, beginning in his childhood and continuing throughout his ministry. These experiences, both comforting and challenging, ultimately served to strengthen his faith and deepen his commitment to his divine mission.

Encounters with the Devil

Throughout history, the Devil has been a persistent force attempting to lead mankind astray. The attitude of a true disciple of Christ must be one of vigilance and strength in the face of this adversary. In today's world, however, the Devil has been largely relegated to the realm of mythology and folklore. Baudelaire wisely observed that the Devil's masterpiece in modern times is convincing people he does not exist. This chapter will detail the many encounters Padre Pio had with the Devil, a force that remains very real and active.

One of Padre Pio's earliest encounters with the prince of evil occurred in 1906 at the convent of Saint Elia of Pianisi. Unable to sleep due to the stifling heat, Padre Pio heard footsteps approaching his room. As he moved to the window, he was shocked to see a monstrous dog with smoke pouring from its mouth. The creature spoke to Padre Pio before disappearing, marking the beginning of a series of battles with the Devil.

Satan tested Padre Pio in various forms, including appearing as young girls dancing naked, a crucifix, Pope Pius X, a guardian angel, St. Francis, and even Our Lady. Padre Pio faced these temptations and attacks with courage, invoking the name of Jesus to free himself. The Devil's attempts to deceive and torment Padre Pio intensified when the saint began to liberate souls possessed by evil.

In numerous letters to his Spiritual Fathers, Padre Pio recounted the Devil's many attempts to harm and deceive him. He described being thrown from his bed, beaten, and spat upon by demonic forces. Padre Pio remained steadfast in his faith and trust in Jesus, Our Lady, his guardian angel, St. Joseph, and St. Francis, who were always with him.

The Devil's deception reached new heights when he appeared in the guise of a penitent seeking confession. In this encounter, Padre Pio ultimately unmasked the deceit by commanding the demon to proclaim the names of Jesus and Mary, causing the creature to vanish in a flash of fire and foul stench.

Padre Pio's encounters with the Devil were not just limited to apparitions; sometimes they took the form of physical attacks. Fellow priest Fr. Perino shared an account of witnessing Padre Pio in the confessional when a dark-haired man entered without waiting his turn. In a moment of divine revelation, Fr. Perino saw Jesus appear in place of Padre Pio before merging with the saint once more. The dark-haired man fell to the ground, defeated.

The many battles between Padre Pio and Satan serve as a reminder that the Devil's presence and influence remain strong in the world. However, through unwavering faith in Christ and the intercession of Our Lady and the saints, we can emerge victorious over the forces of darkness.

Clairvoyance

Padre Pio's extraordinary gifts were a source of wonder and amazement to many. Among them was his ability to perceive things that others could not, often referred to as clairvoyance. This chapter delves into some astonishing accounts of Padre Pio's clairvoyant abilities, which allowed him to read the hearts of those around him and to know of events beyond the ordinary realm of human perception.

In one instance, a spiritual son of Padre Pio, living in Rome, neglected to make his customary small reverence when passing a church due to embarrassment. Hearing Padre Pio's voice scold him, the man later traveled to San Giovanni Rotondo, only to be reproached once more by Padre Pio. This gentle reprimand demonstrated Padre Pio's ability to know of the man's actions, despite the distance separating them.

Another account tells of a man who, upon being sent to retrieve a handkerchief from Padre Pio's cell, took the opportunity to pocket one of the friar's half gloves as a relic. When he returned, Padre Pio thanked him but then instructed the man to return the glove he had taken without permission. His clairvoyance allowed him to know of the man's actions even though he wasn't present.

In yet another tale, a woman knelt before a photograph of Padre Pio each evening to ask for his blessing. Her husband found this practice excessive and would laugh and tease her about it. When the husband mentioned the ritual to Padre Pio, he replied, "I know, I know... and you start laughing." This knowledge demonstrated his ability to perceive the couple's actions from afar.

Similarly, Padre Pio was able to discern the sinful secrets of many who sought his counsel. In one story, a man who appeared to be a good Catholic was secretly unfaithful to his wife. When he attempted to confess a "spiritual crisis" to Padre Pio, the friar immediately confronted him with the truth of his sins, sending the man away in shame. Padre Pio's clairvoyance allowed him to see beyond the man's facade.

Throughout this chapter, numerous accounts reveal Padre Pio's gift of clairvoyance, from knowing the details of a woman's confession even though he initially refused to hear it, to confronting a man about his murderous intentions. In each of these stories, Padre Pio's ability to perceive what others could not is strikingly apparent.

Padre Pio's clairvoyance was not limited to reprimanding and guiding those who sought his help. He also demonstrated his gift in prophetic ways. For instance, he warned a policeman that he would die within eight days, prompting the man to return home to his family. Sure enough, the policeman passed away as Padre Pio had foreseen.

Padre Pio's ability to know the hidden thoughts, actions, and intentions of those around him was a powerful manifestation of his spiritual gifts. These stories reveal how his clairvoyance allowed him to guide, correct, and inspire countless individuals, often leading to profound transformations in their lives.

Confession

The Catechism of the Catholic Church explains the importance of the sacrament of Penance in the life of a believer: "Those who approach the sacrament of Penance obtain pardon from God's mercy for the offense committed against him, and are, at the same time, reconciled with the Church which they have wounded by their sins and which by charity, by example, and by prayer labors for their conversion." The sacrament of confession is an essential part of one's spiritual journey, helping to reconcile oneself with God and the Church.

Padre Pio took this sacrament seriously and emphasized its importance throughout his life. Confession was his principal daily activity, and he had a unique ability to look within the souls of his penitents. This chapter will explore Padre Pio's experiences and teachings on the sacrament of confession, shedding light on the transformative power of this sacred practice.

Padre Pio encouraged believers to approach confession with sincerity and reverence, recognizing that it is a powerful means of conversion and spiritual growth. He advised people to confess at least once a week, as even a closed room needs to be dusted after a week. Padre Pio had little patience for those who approached the sacrament out of curiosity or without a genuine desire to change their lives.

A story recounted by a monk highlights Padre Pio's strict approach to confession. The saint warned a penitent who had not been given absolution that seeking absolution elsewhere without true contrition would result in damnation for both the penitent and the priest. This underscores the gravity with which Padre Pio viewed the sacrament of confession and the need for sincere repentance.

Padre Pio's ability to discern the true state of a person's soul often led to surprising revelations during confession. One man, having completed his confession, was questioned three times by Padre Pio if he had anything else to confess. When the man finally admitted to attending discos, Padre Pio sternly reminded him that dancing can be an invitation to sin. This incident demonstrates Padre Pio's commitment to helping penitents confront their sins and seek true repentance.

Throughout his ministry, Padre Pio addressed various sins that were commonly confessed, including lying, gossip, swearing, missing Holy Mass, practicing magic, divorce, and abortion. In each case, Padre Pio stressed the spiritual consequences of these actions and urged penitents to seek forgiveness and amend their lives.

Swearing, particularly against the Blessed Virgin Mary, was a sin that Padre Pio treated with great severity. He once chastised a man who had cursed Our Lady during a moment of anger, reminding him of the gravity of his offense. Padre Pio also warned against cursing in general, as it can attract the presence of the devil.

Missing Holy Mass on Sundays and holy days was another sin that Padre Pio took seriously. He once reminded a young doctor of the mortal sin he had committed by skipping Mass for a Sunday appointment, emphasizing the importance of attending Mass on such days.

Feast Day and Liturgical Celebrations of Padre Pio

The Feast Day of St. Pio of Pietrelcina, commonly known as Padre Pio, is observed annually on September 23rd, commemorating the day of his passing into eternal life in 1968. As one of the most beloved and venerated saints in the Roman Catholic Church, the Feast Day of Padre Pio is a significant event, marked by various liturgical celebrations and devotional practices across the world. This chapter explores the importance of Padre Pio's Feast Day and the ways in which his life and legacy are honored through liturgical celebrations.

Significance of the Feast Day

The Feast Day of a saint is an opportunity for the faithful to reflect on the saint's life, virtues, and teachings. In the case of Padre Pio, his Feast Day invites believers to contemplate his unwavering faith, commitment to prayer, and love for God and neighbor. Padre Pio's Feast Day also serves as a reminder of the power of intercessory prayer and the importance of seeking the guidance and assistance of the saints in our spiritual journey.

Holy Mass

The central liturgical celebration on the Feast Day of Padre Pio is the Holy Mass. Churches across the world hold special Masses in honor of Padre Pio, where the faithful come together to give thanks for his intercession, seek his guidance, and ask for his prayers. During these Masses, the readings, prayers, and homilies often focus on Padre Pio's life and the virtues he embodied, encouraging the faithful to imitate his example and grow in holiness.

Novenas and Prayers

In the days leading up to Padre Pio's Feast Day, many devotees engage in a novena, a nine-day period of prayer, to seek his intercession and prepare spiritually for the Feast Day. The prayers of the novena often include petitions for healing, conversion, and strength in times of trial, reflecting Padre Pio's own ministry and the miracles attributed to his intercession.

On the Feast Day itself, believers may recite special prayers in honor of Padre Pio, such as the Litany of St. Pio of Pietrelcina, the Chaplet of Padre Pio, or the Prayer to St. Pio for Healing.

Processions and Veneration of Relics

In some regions, particularly in Italy and the hometown of San Giovanni Rotondo, where Padre Pio lived and served, the Feast Day is marked by solemn processions. These processions involve carrying statues, icons, or relics of Padre Pio through the streets, accompanied by prayers, hymns, and moments of silent reflection.

The veneration of Padre Pio's relics is another significant aspect of the Feast Day celebrations. Believers may visit churches or shrines housing his relics to offer prayers and seek his intercession. In some cases, the relics may be made available for public veneration during special liturgical services or devotional activities.

Acts of Charity and Service

In keeping with Padre Pio's commitment to serving the

poor, the sick, and the marginalized, many devotees choose to mark his Feast Day by engaging in acts of charity and service. This may include volunteering at local shelters or soup kitchens, visiting the sick and elderly, or donating to charitable organizations associated with Padre Pio's legacy, such as the hospitals and medical facilities he founded or supported.

In conclusion, the Feast Day of Padre Pio is a time for believers to come together in prayer, reflection, and action, drawing inspiration from his life and teachings. Through liturgical celebrations and devotional practices, the faithful are encouraged to grow in holiness and deepen their relationship with God, following the example of St. Pio of Pietrelcina. By venerating Padre Pio on his Feast Day and throughout the year, believers can find strength and guidance in their spiritual journey, and be reminded of the transformative power of faith, prayer, and selfless service to others.

Educational and Cultural Events

In addition to the liturgical and devotional practices, some communities host educational and cultural events in honor of Padre Pio on his Feast Day. These events may include workshops, seminars, and discussions on Padre Pio's life, teachings, and spiritual insights. Film screenings, exhibitions, and performances that highlight his life and legacy may also take place, engaging a broader audience and fostering a deeper appreciation for Padre Pio's impact on the Church and the world.

Pilgrimages

Many devotees of Padre Pio choose to undertake pilgrimages to sites associated with his life and ministry as a way to honor him on his Feast Day. The primary destination for these pilgrimages is the town of San Giovanni Rotondo in Italy, where Padre Pio lived for most of his life, and where his body is entombed in the Shrine of St. Pio. Pilgrims may also visit the nearby town of Pietrelcina, Padre Pio's birthplace, and other sites connected to his life and work.

These pilgrimages offer believers the opportunity to walk in the footsteps of Padre Pio, deepen their understanding of his life, and draw inspiration from the sacred sites associated with his ministry. They also provide a chance for spiritual renewal, reflection, and prayer, as well as fellowship with other devotees of Padre Pio.

Sharing Stories of Padre Pio's Intercession

One of the most meaningful ways to celebrate Padre Pio's Feast Day is to share personal stories and testimonies of his intercession. Believers can recount their experiences of answered prayers, healing, and spiritual guidance attributed to Padre Pio's intercession, either in person or through social media and other platforms. These testimonies serve to strengthen the faith of others, inspire devotion to Padre Pio, and bear witness to the power of prayer and the loving presence of the saints in our lives.

By participating in these various Feast Day and liturgical celebrations, believers can deepen their connection to

Padre Pio, draw inspiration from his life and virtues, and be encouraged to grow in holiness and love for God and neighbor.

Prayers and Devotions

Healing Prayers

Padre Pio is widely known for his ability to heal people, both physically and spiritually. Many people pray to him for healing from illnesses and diseases, as well as for emotional and spiritual healing.

Prayer to Padre Pio for Health

Heavenly Father, in the name of Jesus, we come before You with humble hearts, seeking Your healing and mercy. We turn to Your faithful servant, Padre Pio, who was anointed with the gift of healing and the power to comfort those in pain and suffering.

Padre Pio, intercede for us, as we place our trust in your compassion and intercessory prayers. We come to you with our infirmities, whether they are physical, emotional, or spiritual, and ask for your powerful intervention in our lives.

Padre Pio, please pray for us that the Lord will grant us the strength to endure our trials, the wisdom to understand our purpose, and the courage to persevere in faith. May our pain and suffering be transformed into a source of growth, wisdom, and grace.

We ask for your prayers, Padre Pio, that our hearts may be open to God's healing touch. Guide our minds to seek His will in our lives, and lead our souls to the refuge of His loving embrace.

Please pray for us that our faith may be strengthened, and that we may find solace in the Lord's presence. May we be reminded that we are never alone, for He is always by our side, walking with us through our darkest moments.

Padre Pio, through your intercession, we ask that God's healing power be poured upon us. May His divine love and grace fill our hearts and renew our spirits. We trust in His infinite mercy and the hope of eternal salvation.

In the name of Jesus, we place our hope and trust in the healing power of His love. Amen.

Prayer to Padre Pio for Renewal and Restoration

Oh gracious Lord, our Refuge and Healer, we come to You with open hearts, seeking Your divine intervention and healing in our lives. We invoke the powerful intercession of Your servant, Padre Pio, who was blessed with the gift of healing the sick and wounded in body, mind, and spirit.

Padre Pio, we beseech you, pray for us in our time of need. We place before you our burdens, our illnesses, our brokenness, and our wounded souls. We ask for your guidance, protection, and assistance as we navigate the storms of life.

Through your prayers, Padre Pio, may we find solace in the Lord's tender embrace, trusting in His boundless love and mercy. We ask that our hearts be filled with the Holy Spirit, granting us the courage to face our challenges and the wisdom to discern God's will.

Padre Pio, intercede for us, that we may experience God's healing presence, mending our bodies, restoring our minds, and renewing our spirits. May our suffering be transformed into a testament of faith and a witness to God's miraculous power.

We pray that the Lord will grant us the strength to persevere through our trials, to uplift others with compassion and kindness, and to walk in the light of His grace. Padre Pio, through your intercession, may we be reminded that in the midst of our pain, we are never alone, for the Lord is our constant companion and guide.

In the name of Jesus Christ, our Savior and Redeemer, we place our trust in the loving hands of the Almighty, confident in His healing power and unwavering love. Amen.

Prayer to Padre Pio for Inner Peace and Healing

Dearest Lord, our Shelter and Salvation, we come before You with humility and a longing for Your healing grace. We implore the intercession of Your devoted servant, Padre Pio, who has touched the lives of many through his miraculous gift of healing and his unwavering faith.

Padre Pio, we humbly ask for your prayers on our behalf as we seek healing from the physical, emotional, and spiritual wounds that afflict us. Please present our petitions to the Lord, trusting in His boundless love and endless mercy.

Through your intercession, Padre Pio, may we find solace in the Lord's infinite wisdom and be guided by His gentle hand. We ask that He fill our hearts with His Holy Spirit, granting us the inner peace and serenity we long for.

Padre Pio, pray for us that we may experience God's healing embrace, as He mends our broken bodies, soothes our troubled minds, and rekindles our weary spirits. May our suffering be a catalyst for spiritual growth, and may we emerge stronger, more resilient, and ever closer to our

Heavenly Father.

We pray that the Lord will fortify us with the courage to face our challenges, the compassion to comfort others in need, and the wisdom to walk in His light. Padre Pio, through your intercession, remind us that in our darkest moments, the Lord is our unwavering source of strength, guidance, and love.

In the name of Jesus Christ, our Savior and Redeemer, we place our trust in the healing power of God's divine love, confident that His presence will guide us towards wholeness and peace. Amen.

Family & Relationship Prayers

Padre Pio believed that the family was the foundation of society, and he often prayed for families and relationships. People pray to him for guidance in their family life, and for reconciliation and healing in broken relationships.

Prayer to Padre Pio for Unity and Love in Families

Heavenly Father, the source of all love and goodness, we come before You seeking Your guidance and grace in our family life. We call upon the intercession of Your faithful servant, Padre Pio, who believed in the sanctity of family and the importance of strong relationships.

Padre Pio, please pray for our family and for families everywhere. We ask that you present our petitions to the Lord, who knows the deepest desires of our hearts. Help us to nurture a home filled with love, understanding, and forgiveness, where each member finds support and encouragement.

Through your intercession, Padre Pio, we ask the Lord to bestow His blessings upon our family, that we may grow in faith and love for one another. May He strengthen the bonds between us, healing any wounds or misunderstandings that have caused pain and division.

Padre Pio, pray for us that our family may be a living testimony of God's grace and mercy. May we be examples of kindness, generosity, and compassion to those around us, and may we extend our love beyond the walls of our home to touch the lives of others.

We pray that the Lord will protect and guide our family, providing us with wisdom and discernment in navigating life's challenges. Padre Pio, through your intercession, may we find comfort in knowing that the Lord is our refuge, and that He is always present in our family life.

In the name of Jesus Christ, our Savior and Redeemer, we place our trust in the divine love of our Heavenly Father, who has blessed us with the gift of family. May His grace continue to strengthen, unite, and guide us on our journey together. Amen.

Prayer to Padre Pio for Reconciliation and Forgiveness in Relationships

Loving Father, the wellspring of grace and mercy, we approach You with humble hearts, seeking Your guidance and healing in our relationships. We invoke the intercession of Your devoted servant, Padre Pio, who cherished the importance of family and understood the value of true connection.

Padre Pio, we ask for your prayers as we seek reconciliation and forgiveness in our relationships. Please bring our concerns to the Lord, who knows our hearts and longs to restore harmony and love in our lives.

Through your intercession, Padre Pio, we pray that the Lord will grant us the humility to recognize our own faults and the willingness to forgive those who have hurt us. May He soften our hearts, allowing us to release any bitterness or resentment that has taken root within.

Padre Pio, pray for us that we may cultivate a spirit of understanding, empathy, and patience with one another. May our relationships be a reflection of God's love, and may we strive to support, uplift, and cherish each other in both times of joy and times of sorrow.

We ask that the Lord will bless and protect our relationships, guiding us through the complexities of life with wisdom and grace. Padre Pio, through your intercession, remind us that the Lord is our constant source of strength, healing, and unity in all aspects of our lives.

In the name of Jesus Christ, our Savior and Redeemer, we place our trust in the healing power of God's love, confident that His presence will mend our brokenness and restore harmony in our relationships. Amen.

Prayer to Padre Pio for Wisdom and Guidance in Family Life

Almighty Father, the source of all wisdom and understanding, we come before You in search of guidance and direction in our family life. We ask for the intercession of Your compassionate servant, Padre Pio, who recognized the importance of family as the cornerstone of society and dedicated his life to strengthening the bonds of love.

Padre Pio, we beseech you to pray for us as we strive to create a loving and nurturing environment in our homes. Bring our petitions before the Lord, who understands the complexities of family life and desires for us to grow in love and unity.

Through your intercession, Padre Pio, we ask the Lord to grant us the wisdom to navigate the challenges that arise within our families. May He help us to create a home where love, respect, and understanding are the foundations upon which we build our relationships.

Padre Pio, pray for us that we may learn to communicate openly and honestly with one another, fostering a spirit of trust and cooperation. May our family be a sanctuary of support and encouragement, where each member is cherished and valued.

We ask the Lord to watch over our family, providing us with the guidance and discernment needed to grow in faith and love. Padre Pio, through your intercession, remind us that the Lord is our refuge and our strength, ever-present in our family life.

In the name of Jesus Christ, our Savior and Redeemer, we place our trust in the divine wisdom of our Heavenly Father, confident that His love and grace will guide us through the journey of family life. Amen.

Spiritual Growth Prayers

Padre Pio was a great spiritual director, and he helped many people on their spiritual journey. People pray to him for guidance in their spiritual growth, and for the grace to live a holy and virtuous life.

Prayer to Padre Pio for Spiritual Growth and Holiness

Heavenly Father, the fountain of all wisdom and grace, we approach You with hearts yearning for spiritual growth and a deeper relationship with You. We call upon the intercession of Your humble servant, Padre Pio, who was a beacon of holiness and an exemplary spiritual guide.

Padre Pio, we ask for your prayers as we embark on our journey towards greater spiritual maturity. Present our petitions to the Lord, who knows our deepest desires and longs to nourish our souls with His divine presence.

Through your intercession, Padre Pio, we pray that the Lord will grant us the grace to grow in humility, patience, and self-control. May He strengthen our faith, increase our hope, and inflame our hearts with divine love.

Padre Pio, pray for us that we may develop a deeper prayer life, seeking solace and guidance in the Lord's presence. May we cultivate an attitude of gratitude and a spirit of generosity, sharing the gifts we have received with those in need.

We ask that the Lord will guide us on the path of holiness, inspiring us to follow the example of Jesus Christ, our Savior and Redeemer. Padre Pio, through your intercession, may we be reminded that the Lord is our ever-present companion, walking with us on our spiritual journey.

In the name of Jesus Christ, we place our trust in the grace of our Heavenly Father, confident that His love and guidance will lead us to spiritual growth and a virtuous life. Amen.

Prayer to Padre Pio for Discernment and Spiritual Progress

Eternal Father, the source of all truth and sanctity, we come before You with a longing to deepen our spiritual lives and to draw closer to You. We seek the intercession of Your faithful servant, Padre Pio, who devoted his life to guiding souls on the path to holiness and spiritual growth.

Padre Pio, please pray for us as we strive to advance in our spiritual journey. Present our petitions to the Lord, who knows our hearts and desires to draw us into a more intimate relationship with Him.

Through your intercession, Padre Pio, we ask the Lord to gift us with discernment, that we may recognize His voice and follow His gentle guidance. May He instill in us a hunger for righteousness, a thirst for knowledge, and a desire for deeper prayer and contemplation.

Padre Pio, pray for us that we may become more like Christ in our words, actions, and thoughts. May we develop a spirit of humility, kindness, and selflessness, bearing witness to God's love and mercy in our daily lives.

We pray that the Lord will grant us the grace to persevere in our spiritual journey, even in the face of obstacles and setbacks. Padre Pio, through your intercession, remind us that the Lord is our constant source of strength, wisdom, and inspiration as we progress along the path of holiness.

In the name of Jesus Christ, our Savior and Redeemer, we place our trust in the guidance and grace of our Heavenly Father, confident that His love and mercy will lead us to spiritual growth and a life of virtue. Amen.

Prayer to Padre Pio for Surrender and Trust in Our Spiritual Journey

Almighty Father, the wellspring of grace and love, we approach You with open hearts, yearning to grow closer to You and progress on our spiritual journey. We seek the intercession of Your devoted servant, Padre Pio, who guided countless souls towards holiness and deeper communion with You.

Padre Pio, we implore your prayers as we strive to surrender our lives more fully to the Lord. Bring our petitions before Him, who knows our innermost thoughts and longs to fill our hearts with His divine presence.

Through your intercession, Padre Pio, we pray that the Lord will teach us to trust in His providence and to place our lives entirely in His hands. May He grant us the grace to be open to His will, allowing ourselves to be guided by His gentle whispers and loving embrace.

Padre Pio, pray for us that we may find solace and strength in the Lord's presence, knowing that He is our refuge and our fortress. May we cultivate a spirit of prayer, seeking His wisdom and guidance as we navigate the complexities of life.

We ask the Lord to help us grow in holiness, shaping our hearts to be more like His, filled with love, mercy, and compassion. Padre Pio, through your intercession, remind us that the Lord is our shepherd, leading us on the path of righteousness and sanctity.

In the name of Jesus Christ, our Savior and Redeemer, we place our trust in the loving arms of our Heavenly Father, confident that His grace and guidance will sustain us on our spiritual journey towards eternal life. Amen.

Financial Prayers

Padre Pio was known to have helped many people in financial difficulty. People pray to him for assistance with their financial struggles, and for the wisdom and resources to manage their finances wisely.

Prayer to Padre Pio for Financial Wisdom and Assistance

Heavenly Father, the provider of all our needs, we come before You with humble hearts, seeking Your guidance and blessings in our financial lives. We ask for the intercession of Your devoted servant, Padre Pio, who offered hope and support to those facing financial difficulties.

Padre Pio, please pray for us as we navigate our financial challenges. Present our petitions to the Lord, who knows our struggles and desires to bless us with abundance and security.

Through your intercession, Padre Pio, we ask the Lord to grant us the wisdom to manage our finances responsibly and to make prudent decisions in our stewardship. May He provide us with the resources we need to meet our obligations and care for our families.

Padre Pio, pray for us that we may learn to trust in the Lord's providence and to recognize His hand in all aspects of our lives, including our financial well-being. May we cultivate a spirit of gratitude for the blessings we have received and a heart of generosity toward those in need.

We ask the Lord to guide and protect us in our financial

endeavors, granting us the strength to persevere through uncertainty and setbacks. Padre Pio, through your intercession, remind us that our true wealth lies in the love and grace of our Heavenly Father, who provides for us in abundance.

In the name of Jesus Christ, our Savior and Redeemer, we place our trust in the divine providence of our Heavenly Father, confident that His love and wisdom will guide us through our financial struggles and lead us to a life of abundance and peace. Amen.

Prayer to Padre Pio for Financial Stability and Trust in God's Providence

Almighty Father, the giver of every good gift, we approach You in our time of need, seeking Your divine assistance in our financial struggles. We ask for the intercession of Your loving servant, Padre Pio, who offered solace and aid to those facing financial challenges.

Padre Pio, we implore your prayers on our behalf as we navigate our financial circumstances. Bring our concerns before the Lord, who knows our burdens and desires to shower us with His grace and blessings.

Through your intercession, Padre Pio, we pray that the Lord will grant us the wisdom to discern the best course of action in managing our finances. May He bless us with the resources necessary to provide for our needs and the needs of our loved ones.

Padre Pio, pray for us that we may develop a deeper trust in God's providence and recognize His presence in every aspect of our lives, including our financial well-being. May we learn to be grateful for the gifts we have received and to share our blessings with those who are less fortunate.

We ask the Lord to guide us in our financial decisions, providing us with the strength and perseverance needed to face any challenges that may arise. Padre Pio, through your intercession, remind us that our true treasure lies not in material wealth but in the boundless love and mercy of our Heavenly Father.

In the name of Jesus Christ, our Savior and Redeemer, we place our trust in the divine providence of our Heavenly Father, confident that His love and guidance will lead us to financial stability and a life of peace and abundance. Amen.

Prayer to Padre Pio for Financial Relief and Responsible Stewardship

Gracious Father, the sustainer of our lives and the source of all blessings, we turn to You in our time of financial need, seeking Your guidance and provision. We ask for the intercession of Your faithful servant, Padre Pio, who brought comfort and help to those facing financial hardships.

Padre Pio, please pray for us as we confront our financial difficulties. Present our petitions to the Lord, who knows our anxieties and longs to provide for us in our times of struggle.

Through your intercession, Padre Pio, we ask the Lord to bestow upon us the wisdom to manage our finances wisely and to make responsible decisions in our stewardship. May

He supply us with the resources we need to meet our responsibilities and to support our families.

Padre Pio, pray for us that we may place our trust in God's abundant providence and recognize His loving hand in all areas of our lives, including our financial well-being. May we cultivate a spirit of gratitude for the blessings we have received and a heart of generosity toward those who are in need.

We pray that the Lord will guide us in our financial endeavors, giving us the strength and resilience to overcome any obstacles and setbacks. Padre Pio, through your intercession, remind us that our true riches are found in the love and grace of our Heavenly Father, who provides for us without measure.

In the name of Jesus Christ, our Savior and Redeemer, we place our trust in the divine provision of our Heavenly Father, confident that His love and wisdom will lead us to financial relief and a life of peace and abundance. Amen.

Protection and Safety Prayers

Padre Pio was also known for his protection of his spiritual children. People pray to him for protection from harm, and for safety in their travels and daily lives.

Prayer to Padre Pio for Protection and Safety in Our Daily Lives

Almighty Father, the fortress of our souls, we come before You with humble hearts, seeking Your divine protection and safety in our lives. We ask for the intercession of Your caring servant, Padre Pio, who watched over and protected his spiritual children with unwavering love.

Padre Pio, we implore your prayers for our safety and well-being. Bring our petitions before the Lord, who knows our fears and longs to shelter us in His loving embrace.

Through your intercession, Padre Pio, we ask the Lord to protect us from harm and danger, to guide our steps, and to surround us with His angels as we go about our daily lives. May He watch over our families, friends, and loved ones, keeping them safe from all evil.

Padre Pio, pray for us that we may develop a spirit of courage, trusting in the Lord's protection and the strength of His mighty arm. May we be vigilant in prayer, seeking refuge in God's presence and relying on His power to deliver us from all that threatens our peace and security.

We ask the Lord to guide us in our travels and to protect us in all our endeavors. Padre Pio, through your intercession, remind us that the Lord is our rock, our fortress, and our deliverer, ever-present in our lives and attentive to our needs.

In the name of Jesus Christ, our Savior and Redeemer, we place our trust in the divine protection of our Heavenly Father, confident that His love and grace will shield us from harm and lead us to a life of safety and peace. Amen.

Prayer to Padre Pio for Divine Protection and Security

Heavenly Father, the refuge of our souls, we approach You with trust, seeking Your divine protection and security in our lives. We ask for the intercession of Your faithful servant, Padre Pio, who embraced his spiritual children with love and devotion, ensuring their safety.

Padre Pio, we call upon your prayers for our safety and well-being. Present our petitions to the Lord, who understands our fears and desires to grant us His divine protection.

Through your intercession, Padre Pio, we ask the Lord to shield us from harm, to guide our path, and to surround us with His angels as we journey through life. May He keep watch over our loved ones, safeguarding them from all evil and danger.

Padre Pio, pray for us that we may cultivate a spirit of courage, trusting in the Lord's constant protection and the strength of His powerful hand. May we remain vigilant in prayer, seeking solace in God's presence and relying on His power to save us from all threats to our peace and safety.

We ask the Lord to accompany us in our travels and to protect us in all our undertakings. Padre Pio, through your intercession, remind us that the Lord is our stronghold, our refuge, and our deliverer, ever-present in our lives and attentive to our needs.

In the name of Jesus Christ, our Savior and Redeemer, we place our trust in the divine protection of our Heavenly Father, confident that His love and mercy will defend us from harm and lead us to a life of safety and serenity. Amen.

Prayer to Padre Pio for Shelter from Adversity and Safekeeping

Lord, our mighty shield and defender, we come before You with trusting hearts, seeking Your divine protection and safekeeping in our lives. We ask for the intercession of Your devoted servant, Padre Pio, who tirelessly guarded his spiritual children with compassion and watchfulness.

Padre Pio, we beseech your prayers for our safety and well-being. Bring our petitions before the Lord, who knows our fears and yearns to grant us His divine refuge.

Through your intercession, Padre Pio, we ask the Lord to protect us from all harm, to guide us along our journey, and to surround us with His angels as we navigate our daily lives. May He ensure the safety of our families, friends, and loved ones, keeping them secure from all danger and wickedness.

Padre Pio, pray for us that we may foster a spirit of bravery, relying on the Lord's unwavering protection and the strength of His saving hand. May we stay vigilant in prayer, seeking comfort in God's presence and depending on His power to deliver us from all menaces to our peace and security.

We ask the Lord to watch over us during our travels and to safeguard us in all our endeavors. Padre Pio, through your intercession, remind us that the Lord is our rock, our sanctuary, and our savior, ever-present in our lives and attentive to our needs.

In the name of Jesus Christ, our Savior and Redeemer, we place our trust in the divine protection of our Heavenly Father, confident that His love and grace will shield us from harm and lead us to a life of safety and tranquility. Amen.

Novena

Instructions for Praying the St. Pio of Pietrelcina Novena

1. Set aside a specific time each day for nine consecutive days to pray the novena. It's important to maintain consistency and create a sacred space for your daily prayers. Choose a quiet, comfortable place free from distractions where you can focus on your intentions.

2. Begin each day of the novena by making the Sign of the Cross: In the name of the Father, and of the Son, and of the Holy Spirit. Amen.

3. Recite the prayer for the corresponding day of the novena. There are nine separate prayers, one for each day. As you recite the prayer, meditate on the words and the virtues exemplified by St. Pio.

4. After reciting the daily prayer, say the Prayer to the Sacred Heart of Jesus. This prayer can be a personal prayer or a traditional one, such as: "O Sacred Heart of Jesus, filled with infinite love, broken by our ingratitude, and pierced by our sins, yet loving us still, accept the consecration we make to You of all that we are and all that we have. Take every faculty of our souls and bodies, only day by day draw us nearer and nearer to Your Sacred Heart, and there, as we shall hear the lesson, teach us Your Holy Way. Amen."

5. Offer your intentions for the novena. Take a moment to reflect on your personal intentions or the intentions of others. Consider the virtues of St. Pio and how they may apply to the situation for which you are praying.

6. Conclude each day of the novena with the following closing prayer:

7. "St. Pio of Pietrelcina, pray for us and obtain for us the graces we need to follow your example of holiness and compassion. May your intercession lead us closer to Christ, and may we be inspired by your life to love and serve God and our neighbors. Amen."

8. Make the Sign of the Cross again to conclude your prayer session.

9. Remember that a novena is not a magical formula that guarantees specific results. Rather, it is a powerful way to grow in faith and deepen your relationship with God. Trust in the intercession of St. Pio and the will of God, and be open to the graces and blessings that come from this spiritual practice.

1st Day

Beloved St. Pio of Pietrelcina, you bore the marks of Our Lord Jesus Christ's Passion upon your body. You endured both physical and emotional pain, offering your suffering as a continual sacrifice for all. We beseech you to intercede for us, so that we may embrace the crosses in our lives, both big and small, and offer them to God, securing our place with Him in Eternal Life.

"Embrace the suffering that Jesus sends your way. Jesus cannot bear to see you in pain and will come to comfort you, bestowing abundant graces upon your soul." - Padre Pio

2nd Day

Saint Pio of Pietrelcina, you withstood the temptations of the Devil alongside Our Lord Jesus Christ. You endured demonic assaults and oppression, yet you never abandoned your pursuit of holiness. We implore you to pray for us, so that with your assistance and the aid of the Heavenly Kingdom, we find the strength to resist sin and persevere in our faith until our final breath.

"Be courageous and do not fear the Devil's attacks. Remember this always; it is a good sign if the Devil shouts and roars around your conscience, for it means he is not within your will." - Padre Pio

3rd Day

Virtuous St. Pio of Pietrelcina, your love for Our Holy Mother was profound, and you received daily graces and solace from her. We beseech you to pray to the Holy Mother for us. Place our sorrow for our sins and our prayers of reparation in her hands, so that, as at the Wedding at Cana, her Son grants her request, and our names may be inscribed in the Book of Eternal Life.

"Let Mary be the star that illuminates your path, showing you the sure way to the Heavenly Father. She will be the anchor to which you must cling in the hour of temptation." - Padre Pio

4th Day

Chaste St. Pio of Pietrelcina, you cherished your Guardian Angel, who guided, defended, and relayed messages on your behalf. The Angels brought the prayers of your spiritual children to you. We implore you to pray for us, so that we may learn to call upon our Guardian Angel, who is ever ready to guide us towards goodness and away from sinful deeds.

"Call upon your Guardian Angel, who will enlighten and guide you. God has given him to you for your protection; use him accordingly." - Padre Pio

5th Day

Prudent St. Pio of Pietrelcina, your devotion to the Souls in Purgatory was immense, offering yourself as a victim to lessen their suffering. We beseech you to pray for us, asking God to instill within us the same compassion and love you held for these souls. In doing so, we too can contribute to alleviating their suffering and, through our sacrifices and prayers, obtain the necessary Indulgences for them.

"My God, I beg you, let me bear the punishments prepared for sinners and the souls in Purgatory. Multiply these punishments for me so that you may forgive and save sinners and liberate their souls from purgatory." - Padre Pio

6th Day

Obedient St. Pio of Pietrelcina, your love for the sick exceeded even love for yourself, as you recognized Jesus within them. You performed countless miracles, healing the afflicted in Jesus' name, and granting them peace of mind. We beseech you to pray for us, so that the sick, through the intercession of Mary, may find healing and restoration in their bodies, allowing them to experience the Holy Spirit, and thus offer thanks and praise to God forever.

"If I knew that someone was suffering in mind, body, or soul, I would implore God to set them free from their affliction. I would willingly accept the transfer of their affliction to myself, so that they may be saved and benefit from the fruits of these sufferings... if the Lord would permit me to do so." - Padre Pio

7th Day

Blessed St. Pio of Pietrelcina, you participated in "God's Plan for Salvation" by offering your sufferings to liberate sinners from the Devil's grasp. We implore you to pray for us, so that unbelievers may embrace the faith, all sinners may repent in their hearts, and those with lukewarm faith may rediscover their zeal for a Christian life. Lastly, pray for the faithful, so that they may remain steadfast on their journey toward salvation.

"If people of the World could glimpse the beauty of a soul in God's grace, all sinners and unbelievers would instantly convert." - Padre Pio

8th Day

Pure St. Pio of Pietrelcina, you held immense love for your spiritual children, for whom you shed your blood to draw them closer to Christ. Grant us, who have not met you personally, the privilege of being counted among your spiritual children. In this way, under your protection, guidance, and strength, you may obtain for us a special blessing from God, allowing us to meet Him at Heaven's gates on the day of our death.

"My greatest wish, if it were possible, is that God would grant me this: 'Enter Heaven!' My one true desire is that God would take me to Heaven at the same time as the last of my children and the last of those who submitted to my priestly care have entered." - Padre Pio

9th Day

Humble St. Pio of Pietrelcina, you who loved the Roman Catholic Church, pray for us. May the Master send laborers into the harvest and provide them with the strength and wisdom needed to become children of God. Pray that Our Holy Lady unites Christians everywhere, comforting all within the great house of the Lord, the beacon of our salvation in life's storm, just as a lighthouse guides seafarers to safe harbor amidst a tempest at sea.

"Always remain on the straight and narrow path within the Holy Catholic Church, for She alone is the Bride of Christ and can bring you peace. She alone possesses Jesus in the Blessed Sacrament, who is the true Prince of Peace." - Padre Pio

Afterword

As we reach the conclusion of this exploration into the life and spiritual journey of Padre Pio, it is essential to reflect on his enduring legacy and the impact he continues to have on the faithful worldwide. This humble Capuchin friar from a small town in Italy transcended the boundaries of his time and place to become a guiding light for millions seeking solace, healing, and inspiration in their own spiritual journeys.

Padre Pio's teachings and example have left an indelible mark on the Catholic Church and the lives of countless individuals. His devotion to the Eucharist, the Sacrament of Reconciliation, and prayer, particularly the Holy Rosary, have inspired many to embrace a life of dedication to God.

Decades after his death, the influence of St. Pio of Pietrelcina continues to expand, reaching believers and non-believers alike. His intercession has brought about countless miracles, conversions, and acts of healing. Pilgrims from all corners of the world flock to San Giovanni Rotondo, where his relics and the site of his earthly ministry serve as a testament to his enduring presence.

In this time of uncertainty, where suffering and despair often seem overwhelming, the example and teachings of Padre Pio provide a beacon of hope and solace. His unwavering faith, compassion for others, and devotion to God serve as an inspiration for all who seek to grow in holiness and draw closer to the Divine.

As we close the pages of this book, may the life and legacy of Padre Pio continue to inspire us in our own spiritual journeys, reminding us of the transformative power of faith, hope, and love when grounded in the grace of God.

Appendix

Places of Pilgrimage and Veneration

Sanctuary of Saint Pio of Pietrelcina, San Giovanni Rotondo, Italy: This sanctuary, also known as the Padre Pio Pilgrimage Church, is a modern and architecturally unique church in San Giovanni Rotondo. It was designed by renowned architect Renzo Piano and inaugurated in 2004. The sanctuary holds the relics of St. Padre Pio, including his tomb.

Our Lady of Grace Capuchin Friary, San Giovanni Rotondo, Italy: The friary is where Padre Pio lived for most of his life as a Capuchin friar. It contains his cell, confessional, and other personal belongings. The friary's church, also known as the Church of St. Pio, is where Padre Pio celebrated Mass and heard confessions.

National Centre for Padre Pio, Barto, Pennsylvania, USA: This center is a shrine and spiritual center dedicated to St. Padre Pio in the United States. It includes a replica of the friary and church in San Giovanni Rotondo and houses a collection of Padre Pio's relics and artifacts.

St. Pio of Pietrelcina Chapel, Libis, Quezon City, Philippines: This chapel, located in Metro Manila, is dedicated to St. Padre Pio and serves as a center of devotion for Filipino Catholics.

St. Padre Pio Shrine, Landyshevaya, Belarus: This shrine is the first church dedicated to St. Padre Pio in Belarus, located in the village of Landyshevaya.

Important relics and their locations

Stigmata Gloves: Padre Pio bore the stigmata (the wounds of Christ) on his hands, feet, and side for 50 years. To cover the wounds and absorb the blood, he wore fingerless gloves made of brown wool. These gloves, imbued with his blood, are considered precious relics.

Padre Pio's Habit: The brown Capuchin habit that Padre Pio wore throughout his life as a friar is a relic that symbolizes his commitment to the religious order and his humble lifestyle. Some of these habits are preserved in various churches and shrines dedicated to him.

Padre Pio's Confessional: The confessional in which Padre Pio spent countless hours listening to and absolving the sins of the faithful is considered a relic. It can be found in the Church of Our Lady of Grace in San Giovanni Rotondo, Italy.

Padre Pio's Personal Belongings: Various personal items that belonged to Padre Pio, such as his rosary, prayer books, and the crucifix he used during the Mass, are considered relics. Many of these items are displayed in museums or churches dedicated to his memory.

Padre Pio's Hair: A lock of Padre Pio's hair is considered a relic by some devotees. Preserved in reliquaries, his hair serves as a reminder of his humility and dedication to a life of prayer and penance.

Pilgrimage traditions

Pilgrimage traditions associated with St. Padre Pio have developed over the years as devotees travel to visit the places connected with his life and ministry. These traditions are aimed at deepening one's faith, seeking intercession, and experiencing a spiritual connection with the saint. Some of the most notable pilgrimage traditions include:

Visiting San Giovanni Rotondo: This small town in southern Italy is where St. Padre Pio spent most of his life as a Capuchin friar. Pilgrims visit the Sanctuary of Saint Pio of Pietrelcina and the Our Lady of Grace Capuchin Friary to pay homage to the saint, pray at his tomb, and venerate his relics.

Praying at the cell of Padre Pio: Pilgrims visit Padre Pio's cell in the Our Lady of Grace Capuchin Friary to see the place where he lived, prayed, and experienced mystical phenomena. It is a tradition to pray and meditate in this humble space to draw closer to the saint and seek his intercession.

Attending Mass and Confession: Many pilgrims participate in the celebration of the Eucharist and the Sacrament of Reconciliation at the churches in San Giovanni Rotondo, following in the footsteps of St. Padre Pio, who was known for his dedication to these sacraments.

Walking the Way of the Cross: In San Giovanni Rotondo, there is a Way of the Cross, which is a series of 14 stations depicting the Passion of Jesus Christ. Pilgrims traditionally walk this path, meditating on the suffering and death of Jesus, as Padre Pio himself often did.

Visiting Pietrelcina: The birthplace of St. Padre Pio, Pietrelcina is another popular destination for pilgrims. They visit the saint's childhood home, the Church of St. Anna where he was baptized, and the Chapel of the Holy Family, where he celebrated his first Mass.

Padre Pio Prayer Groups: Many pilgrims join or establish Padre Pio prayer groups in their local communities upon returning from their pilgrimage. These groups are dedicated to praying for the intentions of St. Padre Pio and spreading devotion to him.

Collecting Holy Water and Blessed Oil: Some pilgrims collect holy water from the Sanctuary of Saint Pio or blessed oil from the lamps burning near his tomb. These sacramentals are believed to carry the saint's intercessory power and are often used for personal devotion or shared with others who cannot make the pilgrimage themselves.

Pilgrimage traditions associated with Padre Pio have fostered a strong sense of devotion and spiritual enrichment among the faithful. These practices enable devotees to draw closer to the saint and deepen their faith, seeking his guidance, intercession, and inspiration.

Lessons and Reflections

Padre Pio's extraordinary life was filled with countless moments of divine grace, spiritual growth, and deep compassion. As we delve into his journey, we can draw valuable personal lessons that can inspire and guide us in our own lives. In this chapter, we will explore some of the most significant lessons that can be learned from the life of this remarkable saint.

The Power of Prayer

Padre Pio was a firm believer in the power of prayer. He spent countless hours in prayer, often waking up in the early hours of the morning to begin his day with a conversation with God. From his life, we learn the importance of nurturing our relationship with the divine through prayer. No matter how busy our lives may be, setting aside time for prayer can provide us with spiritual strength and guidance.

The Importance of Humility

Despite the extraordinary gifts that Padre Pio possessed, he never sought fame or recognition. He consistently reminded himself and others that his abilities were not his own but a gift from God. We can learn from Padre Pio's humility by acknowledging our own talents and abilities as gifts from a higher power, and using them to serve others rather than seeking personal gain.

Embracing Suffering

Padre Pio endured immense physical and emotional pain throughout his life, but he never let it deter him from his mission. Instead, he embraced his suffering as a way to grow closer to Christ and unite his pain with that of Jesus on the cross. We too can learn to accept and embrace suffering as an opportunity for spiritual growth and transformation.

Compassion and Forgiveness

As a confessor, Padre Pio showed great compassion and understanding towards those who sought his guidance. He was always willing to forgive and encourage those who were genuinely seeking reconciliation with God. We can take inspiration from Padre Pio's compassionate nature by extending forgiveness and understanding to others, even when it is challenging.

Perseverance in the Face of Adversity

Padre Pio faced numerous trials and tribulations throughout his life, including severe physical ailments, persecution from within the Church, and even accusations of fraud. Despite these challenges, he remained steadfast in his faith and commitment to serving others. We can learn from Padre Pio's example by maintaining our faith and perseverance in the face of adversity, trusting that God will guide and support us.

In conclusion, the life of Padre Pio offers us a wealth of wisdom and inspiration. By embracing the lessons learned from his journey, we can grow in our own spiritual lives and deepen our connection with God. Let us strive to follow in Padre Pio's footsteps, seeking a life of prayer, humility, compassion, and unwavering faith.

Padre Pio's Five Rules for Life

Here are the five rules of life that Padre Pio believed all people should practice:

- Practice Regular Confession: Just as a room gathers dust even when unoccupied, our souls need frequent cleansing. Make it a habit to go for confession at least once a week, acknowledging your mistakes and seeking forgiveness.

- Receive Daily Communion: Recognize that we are all unworthy of the gift of Holy Communion, yet it is God who invites and desires us to partake. Approach the Blessed Sacrament with a contrite heart and a humble spirit, full of love.

- Conduct a Nightly Examination of Conscience: Make it a habit to examine your conscience every evening. Reflect on your actions, thoughts, and words throughout the day, and identify areas where you can improve in order to live a more virtuous life.

- Engage in Daily Spiritual Reading: The power of spiritual reading can inspire significant change and lead individuals towards a path of perfection. Dedicate time each day to read and learn from holy books, nurturing your soul and deepening your faith.

- Practice Mental Prayer Twice Daily: Set aside time for mental prayer twice a day, focusing on your relationship with God and cultivating love for both God and your neighbor. Even if distractions occur or meditation is challenging, persevere and maintain your commitment to this practice.

Popular Quotes

Padre Pio was known for his profound wisdom and spiritual insight, which have touched the lives of countless individuals seeking guidance and inspiration. Throughout his life, he shared numerous quotes that have since become popular and well-loved by his followers. In this chapter, we will explore some of the most poignant and memorable quotes attributed to Padre Pio, as well as provide context to better understand their significance in his life and teachings.

"Pray, hope, and don't worry. Worry is useless. God is merciful and will hear your prayer."

This famous quote from Padre Pio serves as a gentle reminder of the importance of faith and trust in God's providence. It emphasizes the need to maintain hope and let go of worry, as worry only hinders our connection with God.

"The most beautiful act of faith is the one made in darkness, in sacrifice, and with extreme effort."

Padre Pio recognized that true faith is not always easy. This quote highlights the beauty and merit of maintaining faith even when faced with adversity, doubt, or darkness, as it is in these moments that we can grow spiritually.

"Love our Lady, and make her loved; always recite the Rosary and recite it as often as possible."

Padre Pio had a deep devotion to the Virgin Mary and the power of the Rosary. In this quote, he encourages others to foster a love for Mary and to find solace and strength in praying the Rosary.

"My past, O Lord, to Your mercy; my present, to Your love; my future, to Your providence."

This prayerful quote expresses Padre Pio's unwavering faith in God's mercy, love, and guidance. It is a powerful statement of surrender and trust in the divine plan for one's life.

"Have courage and do not fear the assaults of the Devil. Remember this forever; it is a healthy sign if the devil shouts and roars around your conscience since this shows that he is not inside your will."

Padre Pio acknowledged the reality of spiritual warfare and the presence of evil in the world. However, in this quote, he reassures us that if we are facing opposition from the Devil, it is a sign that we are on the right path and that our will is aligned with God's.

Thank you!

We greatly value your feedback on this book and invite you to share your thoughts with us. As a growing independent publishing company, we are constantly striving to enhance the quality of our publications.

To make it easy for you to provide your insights, the QR code located to the right will directly lead you to the Amazon review page, where you can share your experience and offer any suggestions for improvement that you may have.

Related books

Scan the QR code below to browse our selection of related books and access exclusive supplemental materials:

Made in the USA
Las Vegas, NV
12 May 2023